MIND BENDERS®
DEDUCTIVE THINKING

SERIES TITLES: WARM-UP MIND BENDERS® ,
MIND BENDERS® A-1, MIND BENDERS® A-2, MIND BENDERS® A-3,
MIND BENDERS® A-4, MIND BENDERS® B-1, MIND BENDERS® B-2,
MIND BENDERS® B-3, MIND BENDERS® B-4, MIND BENDERS® C-1,
MIND BENDERS® C-2, MIND BENDERS® C-3, MIND BENDERS® INSTRUCTIONS
(HOW TO USE CHARTS FOR EASIER SOLUTIONS)

by
Anita Harnadek

© 1978
ISBN-O-89455-020-9
MIDWEST PUBLICATIONS CO. INC.
P.O. BOX 448
PACIFIC GROVE, CA. 93950

TEACHER SUGGESTIONS

PURPOSE

Students having wide ranges of ability, motivation, and achievement seem to be remarkably attracted to Mind Benders® problems. Students who may or may not try to use deductive reasoning for ordinary classwork or homework seem to think Mind Benders® are fun, not work. So the purpose of the MIND BENDERS® series is to give each student what (s)he wants—fun, a happy diversion from routine—while at the same time forcing the student to organize sets of clues—some direct, some indirect—and reach logical conclusions by using pure deductive reasoning.

GENERAL INFORMATION

There are thirteen booklets (also available in duplicator masters) in this series:

WARM-UP MIND BENDERS®
MIND BENDERS® INSTRUCTIONS (HOW TO USE CHARTS FOR EASIER SOLUTIONS)

MIND BENDERS® —A1	
MIND BENDERS® —A2	easy
MIND BENDERS® —A3	
MIND BENDERS® —A4	
MIND BENDERS® —B1	
MIND BENDERS® —B2	medium
MIND BENDERS® —B3	
MIND BENDERS® —B4	
MIND BENDERS® —C1	
MIND BENDERS® —C2	hard
MIND BENDERS® —C3	

Although most of the problems in WARM-UP MIND BENDERS® vary from extremely easy to easy, there are a handful in the medium range. The idea of the problems in this booklet is to give the students practice in using deductive reasoning in very simple situations before presenting them with more clues to use and with clues which are more subtle, as in the other MIND BENDERS® booklets.

Since some teachers will need more problems for their students than other teachers, more than one booklet (or set of duplicator masters) is available in each of the A, B, and C categories. Within a category, there is no substantial difference in difficulty between the booklets offered. (For example, a teacher who needs only 15 problems at the easy level may order any of the four MIND BENDERS® booklets in the A series.)

See the last page of this booklet for general comments about assumptions which can be made from clues in Mind Benders® problems.

HELPFUL HINTS ABOUT SOLVING MIND BENDERS®

Most Mind Benders® in the A, B, and C categories are solved more easily if a chart is used than if the solver simply makes notes about the clues given. To help students solve the problems, nearly every Mind Bender® in these (A, B, and C) booklets is accompanied by a chart made especially for that particular problem.

For a **step-by-step explanation** of using charts to solve Mind Bender® problems, including the way each chart looks after each step, you might like to get the booklet **MIND BENDERS® INSTRUCTIONS (HOW TO USE CHARTS FOR EASIER SOLUTIONS).** Those instructions start with a problem which requires only the simplest chart, and they progress to problems which require complex charts. None of the problems used there is in any of the other MIND BENDERS® booklets.

Basically, however, the instructions (in highly abbreviated form, of course) are these: To fill in a chart, make a notation in each square which is eliminated by a clue. (The notation might be the clue number or the word "no," for example.) When there is only one blank square left in a row (or column) within a category, then "X" that square. Then note the elimination of all the other squares in the matching column (or row). When a chart contains three or more categories, then either the elimination of a square or the "X"ing of a square may also give you more information about previous clues. (For example, if you know that Mr. Brown owns the red car and you have just discovered that the Chevrolet is not the red car, then you have also discovered that Mr. Brown does not own the Chevrolet.)

ANSWERS

SOLUTIONS

Note 1: Each problem has only one solution. If the notation used for eliminations is simply a "no," then the completed chart will have an "X" for each combination named in the solutions given below, and the chart will have a "no" everywhere else. If the notation used for elimination is a clue number, however, then the completed chart may vary from one student to another. (This is because eliminations can sometimes be made in different orders.)

Note 2: If your solutions do not agree with those below, do remember that the instruction booklet mentioned in the "Helpful Hints" section above will give you detailed step-by-step instructions on how to use charts to solve Mind Bender problems.

1. Norma Atley; Leonard Bradley; Kermit Cursen; Marlene Drake.

2. Art, cheerleader tryouts; Brad, play rehearsal; Cindy, math club meeting; Della, baseball practice.

3.

	Dori	Juanita	Leona
music	A	C	B
reading	B	A	C
spelling	C	B	A

4. Asher, dining car waiter, Detroit; Barker, conductor, Chicago; Carson, engineer, South Bend; Mr. Asher, contractor, South Bend; Mr. Barker, attorney, Detroit; Mr. Carson, architect, Chicago.

5. Francesca Ishlan, backgammon; Gretel Loftis, Scrabble; Raoul Korning, Monopoly; Tomio Jones, chess.

6. Archway: Enid, Isaac, Jules. Backster: Debra, Harris, Lila. Crawford: Fern, Grover, Kurt.

7. Alan, Ralph, hamburger, nurse; Bonnie, Troy, eggs, plumber; Cora, Stan, dog food, milk delivery person.

8. Gerald Dorman, New York City, flashlight, work; Lorna Ashford, Trenton, candles, restaurant; Mitsu Elling, Baltimore, kerosene lamp, home.

9. Betty Suzki, carpenter; Cleo Kobyashi, shoemaker; Maxine Wong, plumber; Theodosia Nagese, mason.

10. Jane Irving, pilot, 55; Larry Mendle, drafter, 45; Opal King, test car driver, 32; Perry Nathan, police sergeant, 38.

11. Dawn Qualman, 12, 132 cans, Oddway Road; Europa Sutton, 8, 144 cans, Portland; Franklin Rockland, 11, 110 cans, Marker Avenue; Gin-Tan Talbot, 10, 100 cans, Nesbitt Road.

12.

Name	Home	Tree	Transportation	Vacation
Betty Parter	New York	elm	train	Florida
Doris Honner	Ohio	oak	car	Michigan
Frank Duncan	Kansas	maple	bus	Arizona
Wendy Green	Washington	willow	plane	Mississippi

13. Kinte Wagner, 31, attorney, swimming; Louis Viner, 35, chef, tennis; Manny Zebran, 28, kindergarten teacher, golf; Nathan Younger, 40, jeweler, handball.

14. Marty Tallman, goldfish, 10, condominium, Zephyr; Nora Roberts, canary, 11, apartment, Wagner; Ophelia Usher, dog, 6, house, Yacht; Peter Stevens, kitten, 8, trailer, Vine.

iii

1.

Atley, Bradley, Cursen, and Drake are the married names of Kermit, Leonard, Marlene, and Norma.

1. Drake is Bradley's sister.

2. Cursen is Atley's brother.

3. Norma and Drake are not related.

4. Kermit is a year older than Bradley.

Find the full name of each person.

Chart for problem 1

	K	L	M	N
A				
B				
C				
D				

2.

Art, Brad, Cindy, and Della each had their parents' permission to go to a certain after-school activity today. Find out where each person went (baseball practice, cheerleader tryouts, math club meeting, play rehearsal).

1. Cindy did not go to baseball practice.

2. Brad wanted to go to the cheerleader tryouts but decided to go to a different activity instead.

3. The girl who went to the math club meeting told the club president that the meetings should not be held on the same day as so many other activities.

4. The person who went to baseball practice was upset because she couldn't attend the play rehearsal.

© 1978 MIDWEST PUBLICATIONS CO. INC.

Chart for problem 2

	BP	CT	MCM	PR
A				
B				
C				
D				

3.

Dori, Juanita, and Leona each took three tests today. Each girl got an A on one test, a B on another, and a C on another.

1. Dori's reading grade was higher than Juanita's music grade but lower than Leona's spelling grade.

2. No two girls had the same test grade in any one subject.

Find the grade on each test for each girl.

Chart for problem 3

	Dori			Juanita			Leona		
	A	B	C	A	B	C	A	B	C
M									
R									
S									

4.

Asher, Barker, and Carson work on a train which makes a daily run either from Detroit to Chicago or Chicago to Detroit, both via South Bend. The three men live in the three cities mentioned. Their jobs are conductor, dining car waiter, and engineer.

Three men with the same last names (Mr. Asher, Mr. Barker, and Mr. Carson), who live in the same three cities, are regular passengers on the train. The passengers are an architect, an attorney, and a contractor.

For each man, find his occupation and the city in which he lives.

1. No railroad employee lives in the same city as the passenger with the same last name.

2. The dining car waiter and the attorney are neighbors.

3. Carson lives between the conductor's and Mr. Barker's cities.

4. The architect and the engineer do not live in the same city.

5. The engineer has the same name as the passenger who lives in Chicago.

Chart for problem 4

	Ch	Det	SB	Mr. A	Mr. B	Mr. C	cond	DCW	eng	arch	att	contr
A												
B												
C												
Mr. A												
Mr. B												
Mr. C												
cond												
DCW												
eng												
arch												
att												
contr												

5.

Two girls (Francesca and Gretel) and two boys (Raoul and Tomio) specialize in different games (backgammon, chess, Monopoly, Scrabble). Their last names are Ishlan, Jones, Korning, and Loftis.

Find each person's full name and game specialty.

1. Jones, who does not play Monopoly, and Korning think they are better at their games than the girls are at theirs.

2. The backgammon player said she'd teach Loftis to play Chinese checkers.

3. Gretel and Ishlan had lunch with the Monopoly player.

4. Raoul and the chess player have the same locker in their physical education class at school.

Chart for problem 5

	I	J	K	L	B	C	M	S
F								
G								
R								
T								
B				
C				
M				
S				

6.

For each family, match up the last name (Archway, Backster, Crawford), the mother's first name (Debra, Enid, Fern), the father's first name (Grover, Harris, Isaac), and the first name of the only child (Jules, Kurt, Lila).

In the clues which follow, the last name by itself will refer to the child.

1. Mrs. Archway told Grover that their sons were planning a biking outing.

2. Enid, Debra, and Kurt's mother are on the school board.

3. Isaac, Mr. Crawford, and Lila's father formed a car pool.

4. Crawford and Jules are in different grades.

5. Enid is not married to Harris.

Chart for problem 6

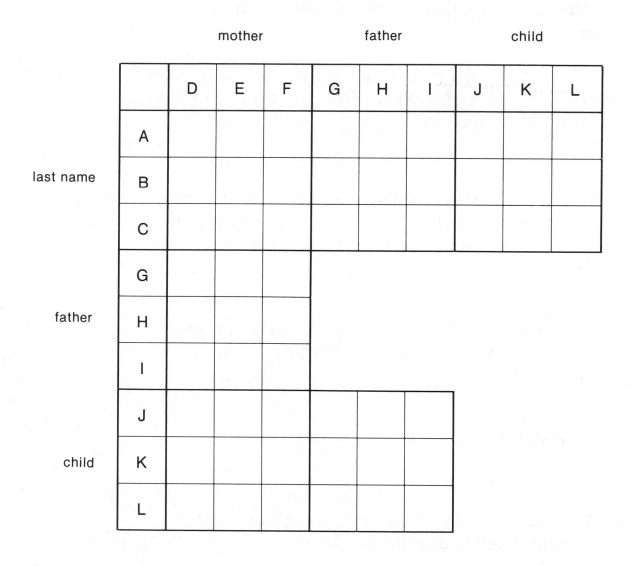

	mother			father			child		
	D	**E**	**F**	**G**	**H**	**I**	**J**	**K**	**L**
A									
B									
C									
G									
H									
I									
J									
K									
L									

last name — A, B, C
father — G, H, I
child — J, K, L

7.

Three children (Alan, Bonnie, Cora) were sent to buy something from the store (dog food, eggs, hamburger) by their fathers (Ralph, Stan, Troy). The fathers' occupations were milk delivery person, nurse, and plumber.

Match up each child with the father, the item the child was supposed to buy from the store, and the father's occupation.

1. On the way to the store, each child forgot what he or she was supposed to buy. Each bought one of the three items, but each bought the wrong item.

2. The plumber's daughter met Cora on the way to the store and bought hamburger.

3. Ralph's son bought dog food.

4. The milk delivery person's daughter was not supposed to buy hamburger.

5. Stan's child was supposed to buy dog food.

© 1978 MIDWEST PUBLICATIONS CO. INC.

Chart for problem 7

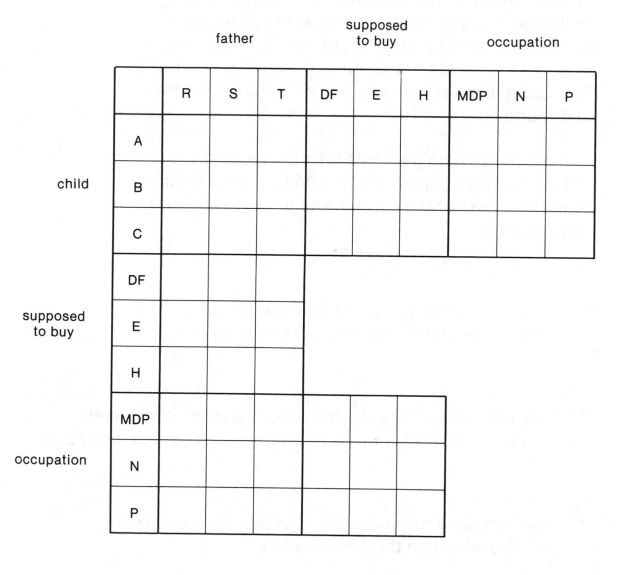

8.

Gerald, Lorna, and Mitsu live in different cities (Baltimore, New York City, Trenton) and were each doing something different (sitting at home, eating in a restaurant, working) when a power failure struck. Each used something different for light (candles, flashlight, kerosene lamp) until power was restored. The last names of the people are Ashford, Dorman, and Elling.

Match up each person's full name with the city, the temporary source of light, and the place (home, restaurant, work) the person was at the time of the power failure.

1. The person who lives in Baltimore, Lorna's sister, did not use candles during the power failure.

2. The man who used a flashlight took longer than the 45 minutes Ashford took to get home when the power failed.

3. The person who lives in Trenton was glad she was not at work when the power failed.

4. Lorna, who was not at home when the power failed, called Dorman to see how he was.

Chart for problem 8

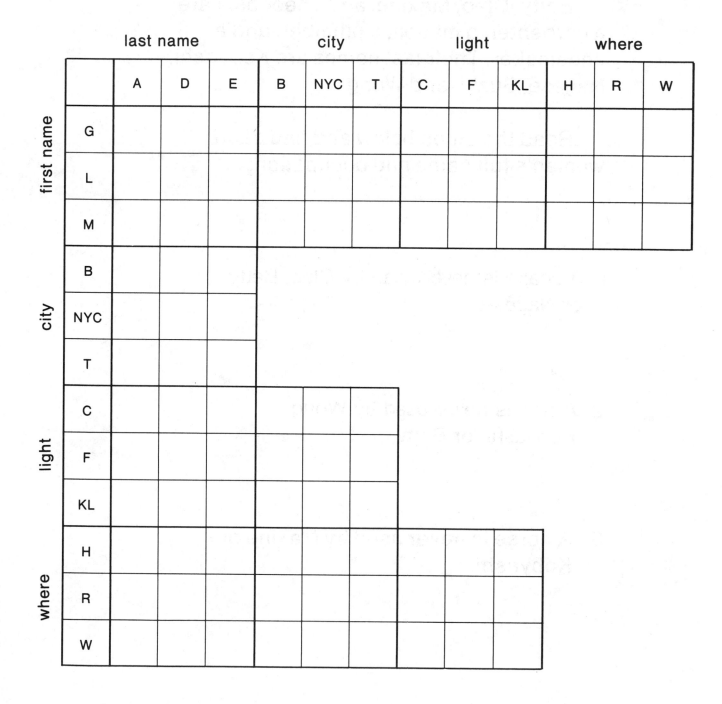

9.

Betty, Cleo, Maxine, and Theodosia are a carpenter, a mason, a plumber, and a shoemaker. Their last names are Kobyashi, Nagese, Suzki, and Wong.

Read the clues below and find each woman's full name and occupation.

1. A snake is never used by Cleo, Betty, or Nagese.

2. A hod is never used by Wong, Kobyashi, or Betty.

3. A horse is never used by Maxine or Kobyashi.

Chart for problem 9

	K	N	S	W	carp	mason	plumb	shoem
B								
C								
M								
T								
carp								
mason								
plumb								
shoem								

10.

A cub reporter interviewed four people. He was very careless, however. Each statement he wrote was half right and half wrong. He went back and interviewed the people again. And again, each statement he wrote was half right and half wrong. From the information below, can you straighten out the mess?

The first names were Jane, Larry, Opal, and Perry. The last names were Irving, King, Mendle, and Nathan. The ages were 32, 38, 45, and 55. The occupations were drafter, pilot, police sergeant, and test car driver.

On the first interview, he wrote these statements, one from each person:

1. Jane: "My name is Irving, and I'm 45."
2. King: "I'm Perry and I drive test cars."
3. Larry: "I'm a police sergeant and I'm 45."
4. Nathan: "I'm a drafter, and I'm 38."

On the second interview, he wrote these statements, one from each person:

5. Mendle: "I'm a pilot, and my name is Larry."
6. Jane: "I'm a pilot, and I'm 45."
7. Opal: "I'm 55 and I drive test cars."
8. Nathan: "I'm 38 and I drive test cars."

©1978 MIDWEST PUBLICATIONS CO. INC.

Chart for problem 10

	I	K	M	N	draft	pol ser	pilot	test dr	32	38	45	55
J												
L												
P												
O												
draft												
pol ser												
pilot												
test dr												
32												
38												
45												
55												

11.

Two girls (Dawn and Europa) and two boys (Franklin and Gin-Tan) worked all day last Saturday collecting canned food for needy families. The last names of the girls and boys are Qualman, Rockland, Sutton, and Talbot, and their ages are 8, 10, 11, and 12. The streets they live on are Marker Avenue, Nesbitt Road, Oddway Road, and Portland. The numbers of cans of food collected were 100, 110, 132, and 144.

Read the clues below and match up everything.

1. Rockland and Gin-Tan's ages are 1/10 as much as the number of cans of food each collected.

2. Dawn and Sutton are Girl Scouts.

3. The boy who lives on Marker Avenue collected more cans than Talbot.

4. The number of letters in the name of Europa's street is the same as her age.

5. Europa is 2/3 as old as, and collected more cans of food than, the girl who lives on Oddway Road.

Chart for problem 11

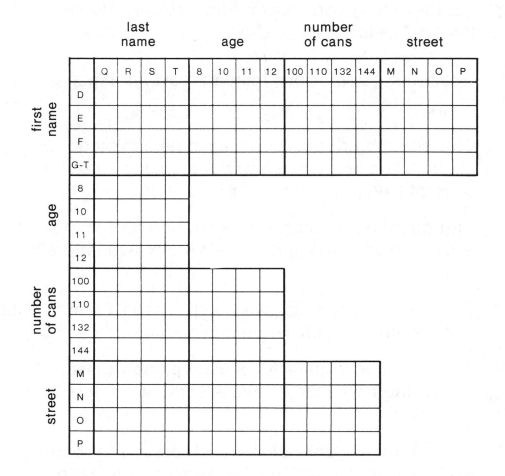

12

Four people whose first names are Betty, Doris Frank, and Wendy, and whose last names are Duncan, Green, Honner, and Parter, live in Kansas, New York, Ohio, and Washington. Each has a different kind of tree in the front yard (elm, maple, oak, willow). Each used a different kind of transportation (bus, car, plane, train) to go on vacation (to Arizona, Florida, Michigan, Mississippi).

From the clues below, match up everything.

1. Not counting duplications, each person's first name has exactly one letter in common with the kind of tree in the front yard.

2. Not counting duplications, each person's home state and vacation state have exactly two letters in common.

3. Not counting duplications, each person's first and last names have exactly two letters in common.

4. Not counting duplications, each person's last name and home state have exactly two letters in common.

5. Not counting duplications, each person's vacation state and front-yard tree have exactly one letter in common.

6. Betty did no go by bus or by plane, and neither did Doris.

7. Parter did not go by car, and Duncan did not go by plane.

©1978 MIDWEST PUBLICATIONS CO. INC.

Chart for problem 12

	Duncan	Green	Honner	Parter	KS	NY	OH	WA	elm	maple	oak	willow	bus	car	plane	train	AZ	FL	MI	MS
home																	**vacation**			
Betty																				
Doris																				
Frank																				
Wendy																				
KS																				
NY																				
OH																				
WA																				
elm																				
maple																				
oak																				
willow																				
bus																				
car																				
plane																				
train																				
AZ																				
FL																				
MI																				
MS																				

13.

Kinte, Louis, Manny, and Nathan are 28, 31, 35, and 40. Their last names are Viner, Wagner, Younger, and Zebran. Their occupations are attorney, chef, jeweler, and kindergarten teacher. Their recreational sports are golf, handball, swimming, and tennis.

From the clues below, match up everything.

1. Kinte is younger than Viner and older than Manny.

2. Zebran, Louis, the attorney, and the oldest of the four men played doubles at tennis yesterday.

3. Nathan and Viner beat the golfer at miniature golf.

4. The attorney and the tennis player are younger than Younger.

5. The attorney is older than the golfer but younger than the chef.

6. The jeweler is older than the swimmer.

7. The chef does not play handball.

Chart for problem 13

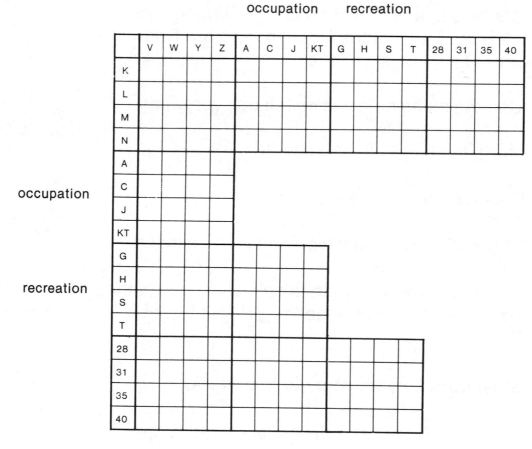

occupation   recreation

	V	W	Y	Z	A	C	J	KT	G	H	S	T	28	31	35	40
K																
L																
M																
N																
A																
C																
J																
KT																
G																
H																
S																
T																
28																
31																
35																
40																

occupation

recreation

14.

Four children (Marty, Nora, Ophelia, and Peter) each have a pet (canary, dog, goldfish, kitten). The children's ages are 6, 8, 10, and 11. They live in an apartment, a condominium, a house, and a trailer. The streets they live on are named Vine, Wagner, Yacht, and Zephyr. The children's last names are Roberts, Stevens, Tallman, and Usher.

Use the clues below to match up everything.

1.   Marty's pet lives in an aquarium.

2.   Roberts' pet sings a lot.

3.   Usher wishes her pet wouldn't bark so much.

4.   Tallman is younger than the girl who lives in the apartment but older than the girl who lives on Yacht.

5.   Stevens is 3 years younger than Nora.

6.   Peter is 4/5 as old as the child who lives on Zephyr.

7.   The dog owner is 3/4 as old as the child who lives in the trailer.

8.   One of the boys lives on Vine.

9.   The house is not on Zephyr.

©1978 MIDWEST PUBLICATIONS CO. INC.

Chart for problem 14

	R	S	T	U	canary	dog	goldfish	kitten	6	8	10	11	apt	cond	house	trailer	V	W	Y	Z
M																				
N																				
O																				
P																				
canary																				
dog																				
goldfish																				
kitten																				
6																				
8																				
10																				
11																				
apt																				
cond																				
house																				
trailer																				
V																				
W																				
Y																				
Z																				

GENERAL COMMENTS ABOUT CLUES IN MIND BENDERS® PROBLEMS

In general, the problems in the MIND BENDERS® booklets assume that you will, when using the clues, apply three guidelines unless a problem leads you to believe otherwise:

1. Think of everyday situations rather than of highly unusual exceptions.
2. Think of standards which are generally acceptable to U.S. society as a whole.
3. Use common sense and context in deciding what the clues mean.

Following are examples:

a. Assume that only males have male names (John, Robert, Dave) and only females have female names (Mary, Jennifer, Cathy). But be careful not to make such assumptions about bisexual names (Pat, Chris, Beverly, Shirley).

b. Assume that the usual U.S. social relationships apply. For example, if John is engaged to Mary, you may assume they know each other. You may assume that very close relatives know each other.

c. Don't assume that rare age relationships may apply. For example, don't assume that a 7-year-old might be a college graduate, or that a parent might be younger than his or her adopted child. On the other hand, although most cases of age may be in one direction, enough cases in the other direction may exist so that these would not be considered especially unusual. For example, a husband may be a good deal younger than his wife, or a 45-year-old may get the mumps.

d. Assume that animals are of normal size. For example, "a horse" is not "a pygmy horse;" "a small dog" is smaller than a goat; a "large dog" is simply one of the larger breeds of dogs. If a problem talks about a cat and a fox, assume that the cat is smaller than the fox. Do not think that maybe the cat is fully grown and the fox is just a couple of weeks old.

e. Assume that animals are called by their usual names within the context. For example, if John and Mary have a pet dog and a pet cat, assume that the cat is an ordinary household cat, rather than maybe a tiger or a leopard.

f. Don't look for tricky situations. For example, suppose the problem has four houses in a row (and no other houses). And suppose Debby lives next door to Gary. Don't assume that Debby or Gary might live in a garage between two of the houses. That is, assume that they live in two of the four houses in the problem.

g. Assume that generally acceptable moral standards apply. For example, if John went on a date with Abbott, assume two things: (1) Abbott is a female, since it is not generally acceptable for a male to "date" a male; (2) neither John nor Abbott is married, since (a) when a married couple go out, we do not call it a "date," and (b) if either one is married to someone else, then it is not generally acceptable for him or her to be dating someone.

h. Pay attention to what the clues say. For example, suppose a problem has four people, and suppose the second clue says, "Cathy and the dentist ride to work together in a car pool." Also suppose the sixth clue says, "Brown, who does not know any of the other three people, is not the typist." Then you should deduce that neither Cathy nor the dentist is Brown.

i. Exact wording to eliminate ambiguities sometimes makes a clue too long. The clue is then shortened to the point where it is unambiguous to most people, but some people would still recognize ambiguities and object to the wording. In such cases, consider the context and the intent of the clue. As examples:
(1) "Neither Bob nor Young lives in the white house," means, "Bob is not Young, and Bob does not live in the white house, and Young does not live in the white house."
(2) "John and Abbott went bowling with Dave and Smith," means, "Four different people went bowling together. One of these was John, one was Abbott, one was Dave, and one was Smith."
(3) "Jane doesn't know either Mary or the artist," means, "Jane doesn't know Mary, and Jane doesn't know the artist, and Mary is not the artist."
(4) "Neither Carol nor Bill went to the party, and Norris didn't go either," refers to three different people.
(5) In general, "neither...nor" and "either...or" sentences will refer to separate things, as in the above examples, Just plain "or" sentences, however, are sometimes less definite, as in this example: "Neither Becky nor Jackson has the dog or is the secretary." Here, Becky and Jackson are different people, but we aren't sure that the person who has the dog is not also the secretary.